THE BIG MISTAKE
WAS STEELING CHARLIE

THE BIG MISTAKE
WAS STEELING CHARLIE

Don't Judge a Book by its Cover

Author: Christopher Chris Zelig

Co-Author: Jennie Zelig

Illustrated by Christopher Zelig

Typewriter Operator: Jennie Zelig

Written in 1987 to comply with a

mandatory third grade homework

assignment.

COPYRIGHT

Dedicated
to my mom
and dad

Illustrated by Chris Zelig

EPIGRAPH

"Never, ever ever ever ever give up."

-Winston Churchill

CONTENTS

ACKNOWLEDGMENTS

This book would have never been enjoyed by dozens of people if it were not for Jennie Zelig, my mother, editor and typewriter operator. Thank you mom. You always were and always will be my hero. I would also like to acknowledge my teachers and staff at Canyon View Elementary School. Thank you for your support and restraint.

1. THE DILEMMA

JACK AND MIKE ARE SMALL TIME THIEVES. THEY HAVE TWO JOBS. ONE
JOB IS A HOT DOG STAND THEY RUN DURING THE DAY. THE OTHER JOB
IS STEALING WHATEVER THEY CAN GET THEIR HANDS ON AT NIGHT.
THEY NEEDED A LOT OF MONEY TO KEEP THEIR HOT DOG STAND AND THEY
NEEDED IT NOW.

Besides adding to the overall girth of the book, this blank page provides space for you to write down all the life changing insights that many people experience after reading brilliant material.

LIFE LESSONS

2. THE LUCRATIVE IDEA

JACK GOT A GREAT IDEA AT THE MOVIES ON HOW TO MAKE SOME BIG BUCKS.
STEAL A KID FOR A COUPLE DAYS, COLLECT THE RANSOM MONEY, THEN GIVE
THE KID BACK. WHAT COULD BE EASIER!

Besides adding to the overall girth of the book, this blank page provides space for you to write down all the life changing insights that many people experience after reading brilliant material.

LIFE LESSONS

3. CHURCH

THEY FIGURED THE BEST PLACE TO FIND AN EASY KID TO DEAL WITH WAS
AT CHURCH SO JACK AND MIKE WENT TO CHURCH FOR THE FIRST TIME IN
YEARS.

Besides adding to the overall girth of the book, this blank page provides space for you to write down all the life changing insights that many people experience after reading brilliant material.

LIFE LESSONS

4. THOU SHALT NOT STEAL

THE CHURCH LESSON WAS ON ONE OF THE TEN COMMANDMENTS, "THOU SHALT
NOT STEAL" WHICH MADE THEM VERY NERVOUS. WHEN THE COLLECTION PLATE
WAS PASSED ALONG THE ISLES MIKE HAD A HARD TIME NOT STEALING THE
MONEY BUT HE REMEMBERED THEY WERE AFTER BIGGER BUCKS.

Besides adding to the overall girth of the book, this blank page provides space for you to write down all the life changing insights that many people experience after reading brilliant material.

LIFE LESSONS

5. EASY TARGET

THEY SPOTTED THE PERFECT KID SINGING IN THE CHORUS. CHARLIE WAS
SEVEN YEARS OLD, HAD RED HAIR, GLASSES AND FRECKLES AND WAS VERY
SMART.

Besides adding to the overall girth of the book, this blank page provides space for you to write down all the life changing insights that many people experience after reading brilliant material.

LIFE LESSONS

CHARLIE WAS WILLING TO GO WITH THEM WHEN JACK TOLD HIM THAT
THEY COULD TIE A ROPE AROUND HIM THAT HE COULDN"T GET OUT OF.
BUT CHARLIE COULD GET OUT OF ANYTHING.

Besides adding to the overall girth of the book, this blank page provides space for you to write down all the life changing insights that many people experience after reading brilliant material.

LIFE LESSONS

7. RANSOM CALL

JACK TIED CHARLIE TO A CHAIR IN ONE OF THEIR ROOMS AND THEY BOTH
WENT TO MAKE THE RANSOM CALL.

Besides adding to the overall girth of the book, this blank page provides space for you to write down all the life changing insights that many people experience after reading brilliant material.

LIFE LESSONS

8. GOOD LUCK

WHEN JACK AND MIKE ASKED CHARLIES PARENTS FOR THE RANSOM MONEY HIS
PARENTS JUST LAUGHED AND SAID GOOD LUCK AND HUNG UP.

Besides adding to the overall girth of the book, this blank page provides space for you to write down all the life changing insights that many people experience after reading brilliant material.

LIFE LESSONS

WHILE THE THIEVES WERE GONE CHARLIE GOT OUT..OF THE ROPES IN SECONDS.
HE LOOKED AROUND THE ROOM AND SAW BOXES OF HOT DOGS AND SAID "WHY
NOT ROAST SOME HOT DOGS". HE COULDN'T FIND ANY WOOD SO HE STARTED
A ROLL OF TOILET PAPER ON FIRE IN A CORNER OF THE ROOM. HE ONLY HAD
TIME TO ROAST TWO HOT DOGS BEFORE THE WHOLE ROOM WAS ON FIRE.

JACK AND MIKE WERE VERY UPSET WHEN THEY GOT

HOME

Besides adding to the overall girth of the book, this blank page provides space for you to write down all the life changing insights that many people experience after reading brilliant material.

LIFE LESSONS

THE NEXT DAY THEY TIED CHARLIE UP AND WENT TO MAKE ANOTHER RANSOM
CALL. THIS TIME THEY ASKED FOR LESS MONEY. CHARLIES PARENTS
LAUGHED AGAIN AND HUNG UP. THEY KNEW THAT STEALING CHARLIE WAS
A BIG MISTAKE.

CHARLIE GOT UN-TIED AND DECIDED TO GO SWIMMING IN THE BATHROOM.
HE PUT TOWELS AT THE BOTTOM OF THE DOOR AND TURNED ALL THE WATER
ON. SOON THE WATER WAS DEEP ENOUGH IN THE ROOM THAT HE COULD
SWIM AROUND. WHEN HE OPENED THE DOOR THE WHOLE HOUSE GOT FLOODED.

WHEN THE THIEVES GOT HOME THEY WERE
VERY, VERY UPSET.

Besides adding to the overall girth of the book, this blank page provides space for you to write down all the life changing insights that many people experience after reading brilliant material.

LIFE LESSONS

11. THE PARTY

THE NEXT DAY JACK TIED CHARLIE UP REALLY GOOD. THEY BOTH WENT OUT
TO MAKE ANOTHER RANSOM CALL. THEY ASKED FOR EVEN LESS MONEY THEN
THE DAY BEFORE. CHARLIE GOT UN-TIED AND DECIDED TO HAVE A PARTY.
HE CALLED AND ORDERED 25 PIZZAS AND CHARGED IT TO JACK AND MIKE.
HE CALLED AND INVITED ALL HIS FRIENDS AND THEY TORE THE HOUSE
APART.

WHEN THE THIEVES GOT HOME THEY WERE VERY,
VERY, VERY UPSET AND WERE READY TO
GIVE UP.

25
PIZZAS
Please

PIZZA
PIZZA
PIZZA
PIZZA

Besides adding to the overall girth of the book, this blank page provides space for you to write down all the life changing insights that many people experience after reading brilliant material.

LIFE LESSONS

12. FINAL OFFER

THE THIEVES MADE ANOTHER RANSOM CALL AND TOLD CHARLIES PARENTS

THAT THEY WOULD GIVE THEM A YEARS SUPPLY OF FREE HOT DOGS IF

THEY WOULD TAKE   CHARLIE BACK.

    CHARLIES PARENTS SAID "WE DON'T LIKE HOT

      DOGS"AND HUNG UP.

    THEIR BIG MISTAKE WAS STEALING CHARLIE

THE END

Besides adding to the overall girth of the book, this blank page provides space for you to write down all the life changing insights that many people experience after reading brilliant material.

LIFE LESSONS

THE END

AUTHOR BIOGRAPHIES

Jennie Zelig

Mother of Christopher Zelig.

Christopher Zelig

Son of Jennie Zelig.

www.ingramcontent.com/pod-product-compliance
Lightning Source LLC
LaVergne TN
LVHW072121070426
835511LV00002B/51